PALM GROWER'S

Beginners Tips And Techniques To Mastering the Art of Palm Tree Cultivation

JESSE WILSON

Table of Contents

Introductory

Depending on the context and location, palm tree cultivation can serve various purposes and provide numerous benefits. Here are some of the reasons why people cultivate palm trees:

• Palm trees are renowned for their exotic and recognizable appearance. They lend a tropical or Mediterranean feel to landscapes and can improve the property's overall aesthetic. Many individuals cultivate palm trees solely for their aesthetic allure.

• Palm trees are frequently employed in landscaping to create focal points, define spaces, and provide shelter. They can be planted strategically to enhance the aesthetic appeal of gardens, parks, resorts, and urban landscapes.

• Some palm tree species, such as the date palm and queen palm, provide excellent shelter and cooling with their broad canopies. In humid climates, planting palm trees strategically can help reduce the heat in outdoor spaces, making them more comfortable.

• In regions where palm trees, such as date palms, coconut palms, and oil palm trees, produce fruit, they can have significant economic value. These trees produce valuable commodities that can be sold for a profit, including dates, coconuts, and palm oil.

• Environmental Benefits Palm trees, like other trees, contribute to the environment by producing oxygen, absorbing carbon dioxide, and purifying the air. In addition, they provide habitat and sustenance for numerous wildlife species.

• In order to stabilize sand dunes and prevent coastal erosion, palm trees are occasionally planted in coastal locations. Their root systems can anchor sand, protecting coastlines from cyclones and rising seas.

• Symbolism and cultural significance are frequently associated with palm trees in many societies. They are associated with vacations, leisure, and idyllic environments. Symbols are frequently employed in art, literature, and religious contexts.

• Some palm tree species are comparatively low-maintenance and can thrive in a wide range of environmental conditions. This makes them a popular landscaping option in regions with scorching and arid climates.

• Palm trees contribute to biodiversity by providing homes for birds, invertebrates, and other animals. Additionally, some palm species produce nectar-rich flowers that attract pollinators.

• Many people merely enjoy having palm trees in their gardens or yards for their own personal enjoyment. The sight and sound of palm fronds rustling in the wind can contribute to the creation of a relaxing and tranquil environment.

It is essential to remember that the suitability of palm trees for a specific location depends on climate, soil type, and available space. It is essential to select the proper palm tree for your specific demands and environment, as different species have different requirements.

Moreover, in some regions, the cultivation of particular palm species may have environmental or ecological consequences; therefore, responsible sowing practices should be observed.

CHAPTER ONE
Choosing The Appropriate Palm Species

To ensure the palm flourishes and meets your expectations, it is essential to choose the proper palm species for your specific location and objective. Consider the following factors when selecting a palm species:

• Climate Compatibility: The local climate is one of the most essential considerations when selecting palms. Different palm species have varying requirements for temperature and humidity. Some are well-suited to tropical or subtropical climates, whereas others are cold-tolerant and can withstand lower temperatures. When selecting a palm species, you should consider the average annual temperature, frost frequency, and humidity levels in your region.

• Choose a palm species that is cold-hardy if you reside in a region that experiences occasional frost or freezing temperatures. Freezing temperatures can cause injury or death to cold-sensitive palms.

• Type of Soil and Drainage Palm trees favor well-drained soil. The type of soil in your area, whether sandy, loamy, or clayey, can affect the growth success of palms. Ensure that the soil's pH is appropriate for the palm species you choose.

• Some palm species thrive in direct sunlight, whereas others favor indirect or filtered light. Consider the quantity of sunlight that your planting site receives throughout the day before selecting a palm species.

• Size and Space: Palm species vary considerably in terms of size. Others can grow to towering heights, while some remain tiny and compact. Evaluate the available space and select a palm species compatible with your landscape design and maintenance preferences.

• Watering Requirements: Palm trees have varying watering needs. Some are drought-resistant and can flourish with minimal watering, whereas others require constant moisture. Consider the water availability in your region and select a palm species that can thrive with the available water.

• Think about your willingness and capacity to care for the palm tree. Some palms necessitate routine pruning and maintenance, while others are more low-maintenance.

- Determine the specific intent behind establishing the palm tree. Are you interested in shade, beauty, fruit production, or something else? Choose a palm species that corresponds with your objectives, as distinct palm species offer a variety of advantages.

- Check with local authorities or homeowners' associations for any restrictions or regulations regarding the planting of specific palm species. Certain palms may be deemed invasive and prohibited in some regions.

- Pest and Disease Resistance: Certain palm species are more pest and disease resistant than others. Choose a species that is less susceptible to the prevalent pests and diseases in your region through research.

• Consider the palm's physical aspect, including its trunk texture, leaf shape, and color, as well as its overall aesthetic appeal. Select a species of palm that complements your landscape design.

Consult with a local nursery or horticulturist who is knowledgeable about palm trees in your region in order to make an informed decision. They can offer advice based on your specific location and landscaping requirements, allowing you to choose the best palm species for your landscaping project.

Planting Your Coconut Palm

It is essential to plant a palm tree properly to guarantee its healthy growth and longevity. Following are the procedures for planting a palm tree:

1. Select the Appropriate Location:

• Ensure that the planting site receives enough sunlight for the palm species you are sowing.

• Consider the space required for the palm tree's mature size.

• Ensure the soil is well-draining and conducive to palm tree growth.

• Determine if any local regulations or guidelines govern the planting of palm trees.

2. Preparing the Ground:

• Conduct a soil test to ascertain its pH and nutrient content. If necessary, amend the soil to suit the palm's needs.

• Dig a trench twice as wide as the root ball, but no deeper than the height of the root ball.

3. Make ready the Palm:

• Remove the palm tree from its container or wrapping made of burlap.

• Remove excess soil from the roots in order to expose the root system.

• Inspect the roots for indications of disease or damage, and prune any diseased or circling roots.

4. The act of planting:

• Position the palm tree in the center of the opening so that the root ball is flush with the surrounding soil.

• Fill the cavity with the amended soil, ensuring that the palm tree is planted vertically.

• Lightly compact the soil to eliminate air pockets and provide stability for the palm.

• Construct a shallow watering receptacle around the palm in order to direct water to the root zone.

5. The act of watering:

• Water the palm tree vigorously immediately after planting to settle the soil and eliminate air pockets.

• Water deeply and consistently for the first few months after planting, keeping the soil consistently moist but not soaked.

• After the establishment period, modify your watering schedule according to the palm species' specific water requirements and the local climate.

6. Apply a layer of mulch around the palm tree's base to help retain moisture, moderate soil temperature, and reduce vegetation competition.

• Keep mulch away from the tree's trunk to prevent decay and parasites.

7. During pruning:

• Prune as necessary any dead or damaged fronds, but avoid removing green fronds unless they are completely deceased. Palms obtain nutrients from their fronds, and excessive pruning can be detrimental to the tree.

8. To fertilize:

• Fertilize the palm tree according to its specific species and age recommendations. Palms typically benefit from palm-specific, slow-release fertilizers.

- Avoid overfertilization, as excessive nutrients are detrimental to palms.

9. Staking (if required):

- In windy areas or for tall palm species, it may be necessary to stake the palm tree until it develops a robust root system. Utilize stakes that are mild on the trunk of the palm.

10. Monitoring and Attention:

- Monitor the palm tree frequently for indications of pests, diseases, and nutrient deficiencies.

- Continue to provide care and maintenance as required, including pruning and fertilization.

Remember that the first few years are crucial for the health and establishment of the palm.

CHAPTER TWO
Palm Tree Services

Palm trees must be properly maintained to ensure their health and attractiveness. Consider the following maintenance duties when caring for palm trees:

• Palms have different watering requirements based on species, age, and climate. It is crucial to water profoundly and consistently, ensuring that the soil is consistently moist but not soggy.

Typically, young palms require more frequent irrigation than mature palms. Avoid shallow, frequent irrigation because it can result in shallow root development.

• Palm trees benefit from regular fertilization, particularly in nutrient-deficient soils. Utilize a balanced, slow-release palm fertilizer or a formulation recommended for your palm species. In the spring and early summer, when the palm is actively developing, apply fertilizer. Overfertilizing can result in nutrient imbalances and excessive growth.

• As necessary, prune palm trees to eliminate any dead or damaged fronds (leaves). To avoid causing stress to the tree, pruning should be performed judiciously and cautiously. Always use clean, pointed instruments to avoid tearing the fronds.

Only the brown, completely deceased fronds should be removed, as the green, healthy fronds provide vital nutrients to the palm.

• Mulching: Spread a layer of mulch around the palm's base to help retain moisture, regulate soil temperature, and reduce vegetation competition. Keep the mulch away from the tree's trunk to avoid decay and parasites. Replace the mulch as necessary.

• Regularly examine your palm tree for evidence of pests (such as palm weevils and scale insects) and diseases (such as fungal infections). Consult a local arborist or horticulturist for appropriate treatment options if you observe any problems.

• Consider using stakes to provide support and stability against high winds and cyclones for palm trees that are tall or newly planted. Utilize materials that will not harm the trunk of the palm, and remove the stakes once the tree has become established.

• If you reside in an area that experiences occasional frost or freezing temperatures, protect your palm tree from frost by wrapping it in frost cloth or burlap during cold spells. In addition, provide additional insulation by mulching the tree's base.

• Inspect the palm tree periodically for signs of stress, nutrient deficiencies, and irregular growth. Immediately address any problems to prevent further damage.

• Palm roots are typically shallow, so use caution when pruning or operating heavy machinery near the base of the tree. Avoid soil compaction, which can damage the root system.

• Consult Local Experts: Consult local arborists, horticulturists, or cooperative extension offices for region- and palm-specific advice. They can offer advice regarding local climate conditions, parasites, and diseases.

Keep in mind that the maintenance requirements of palm trees can vary based on the species and local environmental conditions. Regular monitoring and proactive maintenance are essential for maintaining the health and vitality of your palm tree.

Palm Tree-Lined Landscaping

Palm trees can lend a tropical or Mediterranean touch to your outdoor space, creating a beautiful and relaxing environment. Here are some ideas and suggestions for landscaping with palm trees:

• Choose the Appropriate Palm Species: To begin, choose palm species that are well-suited to your climate and available landscape space. Consider factors such as size, chilly resistance, and maintenance needs.

• Create Points of Interest Palm trees make excellent points of interest in landscape design. As a focal point, plant a solitary palm or a group of palms to attract attention and add visual interest.

• Mix palm species of varying heights and diameters to give your landscape depth and texture. Taller palms can provide shade and a feeling of enclosure, while smaller palms can be utilized as ground cover or as border plants.

• Clustering palm trees together can create a verdant and tropical appearance. Additionally, planting in clusters can protect the landscape from wind and provide privacy.

• Use Varieties of Palm Trees: To add variety to your landscape, combine palm trees of various types. Combine feather palms with fan palms or pinnate palms with palmate palms.

• Consider adding low-growing plants, ground coverings, or ornamental grasses around the base of your palm trees for underplanting. This can lend color, texture, and weed suppression to the landscape.

• Hardscape Elements: Complement the palm trees with hardscape elements such as pathways, patios, and platforms. Natural stone and wood can create a harmonious tropical atmosphere.

• Outdoor Lighting: To create a dramatic effect at night, illuminate your palm trees with outdoor lighting. Uplighting can highlight the trunk and fronds of a palm tree, while pathway lighting can improve safety and navigation.

• Combine palm trees with water features such as ponds, fountains, or pools to create a tranquil oasis in your landscape.

• Create outdoor seating areas under the protection of your palm trees. Install relaxing furnishings, such as lounge chairs and hammocks, to promote leisure.

• Regular pruning and maintenance will keep your palm trees healthy and aesthetically appealing. Remove the dead fronds and examine the plant for signs of parasites or disease.

- Apply mulch around the base of your palm trees to conserve moisture, modulate soil temperature, and improve their overall appearance.

- Integrate colorful accents by means of flowering plants, potted plants, and decorative containers. Add a splash of color to your palm tree landscape with tropical-hued flowers or vivacious containers.

- Create themed gardens, such as a Mediterranean garden or a tropical paradise, by implementing palm trees along with other plants and ornamentation that correspond to the selected theme.

- Drought-Resistant Landscaping: Combine palm trees, drought-resistant vegetation, and xeriscaping principles to create an eco-friendly and water-efficient landscape.

It is essential to consider the overall aesthetics, functionality, and maintenance requirements when designing a landscape with palm trees.

A consultation with a professional landscaper or horticulturist can assist you in making well-informed decisions and designing an outdoor space that complements your preferences and local climate.

CHAPTER THREE
Palm Tree Reproduction Methods

Palm tree propagation entails the production of new palm plants from existing palm plants. There are several methods for propagating palm trees, but bear in mind that palm propagation can be slow and success rates can vary depending on the species. Here are some common techniques for propagating palm trees:

1. Sexual Reproduction (Seed Propagation):

• Collect ripe palm spores from a mature palm tree. The seeds must be completely mature and free of damage and disease.

• Remove any residual fruit pulp from the seeds by cleaning them.

• Soak the seeds in water for two to three days to dissolve the seed coat and promote germination.

• Plant the seeds in well-draining soil, either in pots or directly in the earth, at a depth equal to or slightly deeper than their size.

• Provide consistent moisture and warmth to promote germination, which, depending on the species, may take several weeks to months.

• Transplant the seedlings into individual containers or a suitable outdoor location once they have developed a few leaves.

2. Offspring or Littermates (Asexual Reproduction):

• Numerous palm species produce offsets or offspring naturally at the plant's base. These offsets can be separated with care and replanted as distinct plants.

• Carefully remove the offset from the mother plant only after it has developed a few roots and foliage. Utilize a sterilized, pointed knife or pruning shears.

- Plant the offset in a potting mix with good drainage or directly in the earth.

3.   Cutting   Propagation (Uncommon and Difficult):

- Although it is uncommon, some palm species can be propagated from stem cuttings, although it is more difficult and less successful.

- Allow a stem incision with at least one attached leaf to callus for several days.

- Plant the cutting in potting mix that drains well and provide consistent moisture and warmth.

• This method is not universally effective and may not be applicable to a great number of palm species.

4. Laboratory Propagation via Tissue Culture:

• Tissue culture is a more advanced method suitable for mass propagation and conservation of uncommon or endangered palm species.

• It entails cultivating palm plantlets from microscopic tissue samples in a laboratory setting.

• Tissue culture is generally performed by trained professionals with specialized equipment and knowledge.

5. Air Layering (Infrequently Used):

• Air layering is a technique applicable to certain palm species. It requires creating a wound on a mature stem, administering rooting hormone, and covering the wound with moist sphagnum moss and plastic.

• Once roots have developed, the rooted section can be removed and replanted.

• This technique is uncommon and not appropriate for all palm species.

It is essential to note that palm tree propagation can be sluggish, and it may take several years for the offspring to mature and resemble the parent plant.

Additionally, not all palm species can be propagated using all of these methods; therefore, it is essential to research the requirements and suitability of the palm species of your choice prior to attempting propagation.

Managing Frequent Palm Tree Issues

Pests, diseases, and environmental stressors are a few of the problems that palm trees may face. Here are some common palm tree issues and their solutions:

1. Palm Weevils (Species of Rhynchophorus):

• Palm weevils are destructive insects that infest the palm tree heartwood. Infestation symptoms include wilting, drooping foliage, and holes at the palm's crown.

• Treatment: Early diagnosis is essential. It may be necessary to remove and destroy infected fingertips. Apply insecticides or traps as recommended by local experts as preventative measures.

2. Scale-Like Insects:

• Scale insects can infest palm trees, causing fronds to turn yellow and produce honeydew. On leaves and stems, these pests appear as tiny, round or oval bumps.

• To treat, prune and dispose of infested fronds. To control scale insects, use insecticidal detergents or horticultural oils.

3. Diseases caused by fungi (such as Fusarium Wilt and Ganoderma Butt Rot):

• Fusarium wilt and Ganoderma butt rot are fungi that can cause wilting, decay, and mortality in palm trees.

• Treatment: Once these diseases have infected a palm tree, there is no effective treatment available. Maintaining appropriate soil drainage, avoiding damage to the trunk, and ensuring healthy root systems are all preventative measures.

4. Deficient Nutrients:

• Palms can develop nutrient deficiencies, most frequently magnesium (Mg) or potassium (K) deficiency, which causes yellowing fronds and stunted growth.

• Treat nutrient deficiencies by applying fertilizers tailored to palms that contain the deficient nutrients. Correct soil pH imbalances if necessary.

5. Root Decay:

• Excessive soil moisture can cause root decay in palm trees. Symptoms include yellowing or drooping fronds and an overall health decline.

- Improve the soil's drainage to prevent root decay. Avoid overwatering the palm and plant the root ball above the water table. Early application of fungicides may be helpful.

6. Absurd Pruning:

- Excessive palm frond pruning, particularly of green, healthy fronds, can cause nutritional deficiencies and stunt tree growth.

- Treatment: prune selectively, removing only brown or deceased fronds. Avoid pruning excessively.

7. Frost Damage:

• Cold damage can result in brown or blackened fronds in regions that experience intermittent frost or freezing temperatures.

• Protect palm trees from the cold by wrapping them in frost cloth or burlap during the winter. Use mulch to provide additional insulation at the base.

8. Drought Tension:

• Insufficient irrigation can cause palm trees to experience drought stress, resulting in wilting, yellowing, and leaf drop.

- Treatment: Water palm trees frequently and thoroughly, particularly during arid periods. Mulch the base to retain moisture in the soil.

9. Salt Injury:

- Palms located near saline or subjected to salt spray can develop salt burn, resulting in the browning of their fronds.

- Treatment: regularly rinse salt deposits with clean water. Choose palm species with salinity tolerance for coastal locations.

10. Insufficient Drainage:

• Inadequate soil drainage can contribute to stagnant water around palm roots, causing root suffocation and decline.

• Improve soil drainage by amending the soil with organic matter and constructing adequate drainage channels.

When dealing with palm tree issues, it is essential to accurately identify the problem and take prompt action. Consult a local arborist or horticulturist for palm-specific and regionally-specific advice.

Preventing common palm tree issues through appropriate care and maintenance is frequently the most effective method.

CHAPTER FOUR
Sustainability And Environmentally Friendly Methods

Sustainability and eco-friendly landscaping practices are essential for minimizing the environmental impact of landscaping activities, conserving resources, and creating resilient outdoor spaces. Here are some eco-friendly and sustainable horticulture practices:

• Choose native flora for your landscape design. Native species are adapted to the local climate, soil, and fauna, which reduces the need for excessive amounts of water, fertilizers, and pesticides.

- Drought-Resistant Landscaping: Design landscapes with drought-resistant, low-water-use vegetation. Reduce water usage by incorporating xeriscape principles, such as efficient irrigation systems, mulching, and soil enhancements.

- Install water-saving irrigation systems, such as trickle irrigation or intelligent controllers, to optimize water use. Collect rainwater for irrigation in containers or cisterns. Utilize rain gardens to naturally collect and filter precipitation.

- Improve the health of the soil with organic matter, compost, and mulch. A healthy soil promotes plant growth, increases water retention, and decreases soil erosion.

• Implement integrated pest management (IPM) techniques to reduce the use of chemical pesticides. Encourage pest-controlling insects, raptors, and other natural predators.

• Create wildlife habitats by supplying food, water, and shelter for the native flora and fauna. Utilize native flora and avoid invasive species, which can destabilize local ecosystems.

• Composting: Compost yard waste, leaves, and kitchen refuse to create nutrient-rich compost that can be used as natural plant fertilizer.

• Mulching: Apply mulch around plants to conserve moisture, modulate soil temperature, and reduce weed growth. Utilize organic mulch such as wood shavings or straw.

• Energy-Efficient illumination: Install LED bulbs and timers for energy-efficient outdoor illumination. Use motion sensors or solar-powered lighting to conserve energy.

- Replace impermeable surfaces, such as concrete, with permeable surfaces, such as permeable pavers or gravel, to reduce stormwater discharge and encourage groundwater recharge.

- Reduced Lawn Areas: Reduce the extent of your lawn by incorporating other landscape elements, such as gardens, native plants, and hardscape elements. Lawns require significant amounts of water and care.

- Restore or create natural habitats in your landscape in order to support biodiversity. Create ponds or wetlands, plant trees and vegetation, and provide nesting sites for birds and insects.

• Adopt sustainable maintenance practices, including proper pruning, selective trimming, and minimal pesticide application. Encourage natural processes such as the decomposition of leaf detritus.

• Erosion Control: To prevent soil erosion in sloped areas, use erosion control measures such as erosion mats, vegetative stabilizers, and retaining walls.

• Consider reusing and recycling materials and objects in your landscape, such as reclaimed wood for garden structures and old containers for receptacles. Materials should be recycled whenever feasible.

• Choose sustainable materials, such as reclaimed or FSC-certified wood, recycled plastic, and eco-friendly paving materials, for landscaping elements.

• Share eco-friendly landscaping practices with your community and neighbors to promote sustainable landscaping practices and raise environmental conservation awareness.

By incorporating these eco-friendly and sustainable landscaping techniques, you can reduce your environmental footprint, conserve resources, and create a landscape that is not only attractive but also resilient and in harmony with the natural environment.

Processing Of Palm Products

Palm trees can be harvested for numerous valuable products that can be used for a variety of purposes. The following are common palm products and their methods of harvesting:

1. Elaeis guineensis and Elaeis oleifera:

• Fruit Bunch Harvesting: Palm oil is extracted predominantly from oil palm trees' fruit bunches. Workers use long poles equipped with harvesting hooks to cut palm fruit clusters from the tree. The harvested bundles are then transported to a processing facility.

• Fruit Extraction: The fruit clusters are sterilized, threshed, and pressed in the processing facility to extract the oil. The oil is refined further to generate crude palm oil, which can then be utilized in a variety of products.

2. Cocos nucifera (Coconut) Oil:

• Harvesting Coconuts: coconut oil is extracted from mature coconut meat or copra. Workers use long poles or ascend the trees to harvest mature coconuts.

• Oil Extraction: After harvesting, the coconuts are halved and the flesh is extracted. The meat is then typically sun-dried before being pressed to extract the oil. This oil has culinary, cosmetic, and industrial applications.

3. Phoenix dactylifera:

• Harvesting Dates: Dates are harvested when ripe, typically in late summer or early autumn. To harvest date clusters, workers use long poles or ascend palm trees with long poles.

• Processing Dates: The harvested dates are washed, sorted, and frequently pitted to remove the seeds. They can be ingested fresh or dried and are used in a wide range of dishes and sweets.

4. Palm sugar is produced by harvesting the sap from certain palm species, such as the coconut palm and the toddy palm. Workers cut into the trunk of the tree and capture the sap in containers.

• Boiling and Processing: To reduce the moisture content and concentrate the sugar, the collected fluid is boiled. It is then cooled and formed into blocks or granules for ingestion and sale.

5. Palm Leaves (Different Palm Species):

• Leaf Harvesting: Palm leaves are harvested from various palm species for various purposes, such as the production of woven products and decorative elements in landscaping.

• Drying and Processing: Following harvest, the leaves may be dried, colored, or otherwise processed to prepare them for their intended use.

• Fruit and Nut Harvesting: Some palm species produce edible fruits or nuts that can be harvested for human consumption. For instance, the aca palm (Euterpe oleracea) yields aca berries, whereas the betel nut palm (Areca catechu) yields betel almonds.

• Processing for Consumption: Depending on the species, harvested fruits and nuts are cleansed, processed, and prepared for consumption in a variety of ways.

Noting that sustainable harvesting practices are essential for ensuring the long-term viability of palm tree populations and protecting the ecosystems they are a part of is vital.

Overharvesting and other unsustainable practices can contribute to environmental degradation and biodiversity loss. Numerous regions have implemented regulations to promote the sustainable harvesting of palm products.

Conclusion

Palm trees perform important roles in numerous facets of human existence and the environment. These adaptable trees provide a vast array of goods and services, from sustenance and oil to landscape enhancement and wildlife habitat support.

Understanding the cultivation, selection, maintenance, and sustainable harvesting of palm trees is crucial for optimizing their environmental impact and maximizing their benefits.

Whether you are interested in landscaping with palm trees to create a tropical oasis, cultivating them for their valuable products such as palm oil or coconuts, or simply appreciating their aesthetic allure, you should adhere to responsible and environmentally friendly practices.

As essential components of thriving ecosystems and contributors to our well-being, sustainability and conservation are crucial considerations when working with palm trees.

You can appreciate the beauty and benefits of palm trees while contributing to a greener, more sustainable world by selecting the appropriate palm species for your region, implementing eco-friendly landscaping practices, and adopting sustainable harvesting methods when applicable.

Keep in mind that local knowledge and environmental regulations can provide valuable guidance for the responsible use and management of palm trees in your area.

THE END